"WE ARE THE ONES WE
HAVE BEEN WAITING FOR"

—JUNE JORDAN

Workman Kids
Workman Publishing
Hachette Book Group, Inc.
1290 Avenue of the Americas
New York, NY 10104
workman.com

Workman Kids is an imprint of Workman Publishing, a division of Hachette Book Group, Inc.
The Workman name and logo are registered trademarks of Hachette Book Group, Inc.

Design by Daniella Graner
Cover illustration by Lauren Semmer

The publisher is not responsible for websites (or their content) that are not owned by the publisher.

The Hachette Speakers Bureau provides a wide range of authors for speaking events.
To find out more, go to hachettespeakersbureau.com or email HachetteSpeakers@hbgusa.com.

Workman books may be purchased in bulk for business, educational, or promotional use.
For information, please contact your local bookseller or the Hachette Book Group
Special Markets Department at special.markets@hbgusa.com.

Library of Congress Cataloging-in-Publication Data is available.

ISBN 978-1-5235-2329-0

First Edition February 2025 APS

Distributed in Europe by Hachette Livre, 58 rue Jean Bleuzen, 92 178 Vanves Cedex, France.

Distributed in the United Kingdom by Hachette Book Group, UK,
Carmelite House, 50 Victoria Embankment, London EC4Y 0DZ.

Printed in Dongguan, China, on responsibly sourced paper.

10 9 8 7 6 5 4 3 2 1

For Santi Sunflower
—R.C.

For Hudson
—L.S.

THE ABCs OF WOMEN'S HISTORY

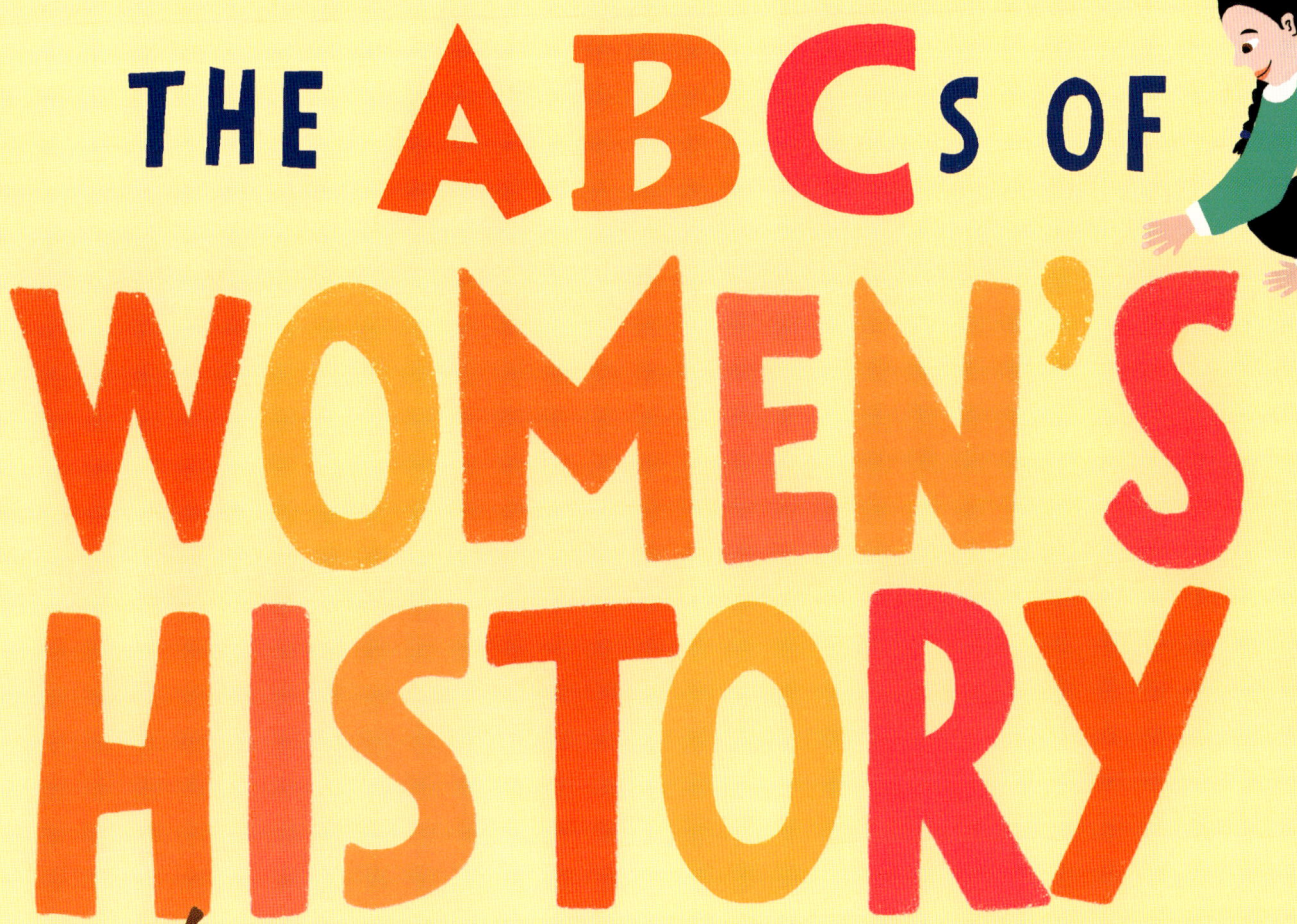

Words by RIO CORTEZ

Illustrated by LAUREN SEMMER

WORKMAN PUBLISHING
NEW YORK

A is for **anew**, we step forward together.
With our history to guide us, we'll make this world better.
As **artists** and **activists**, we've earned our seat at the table.
As **allies** and leaders, we're willing, we're **able**.

A is for **abundance**, and all that we are meant to be.
An **affirmation** to hold:
"I am not just enough, I am plenty."

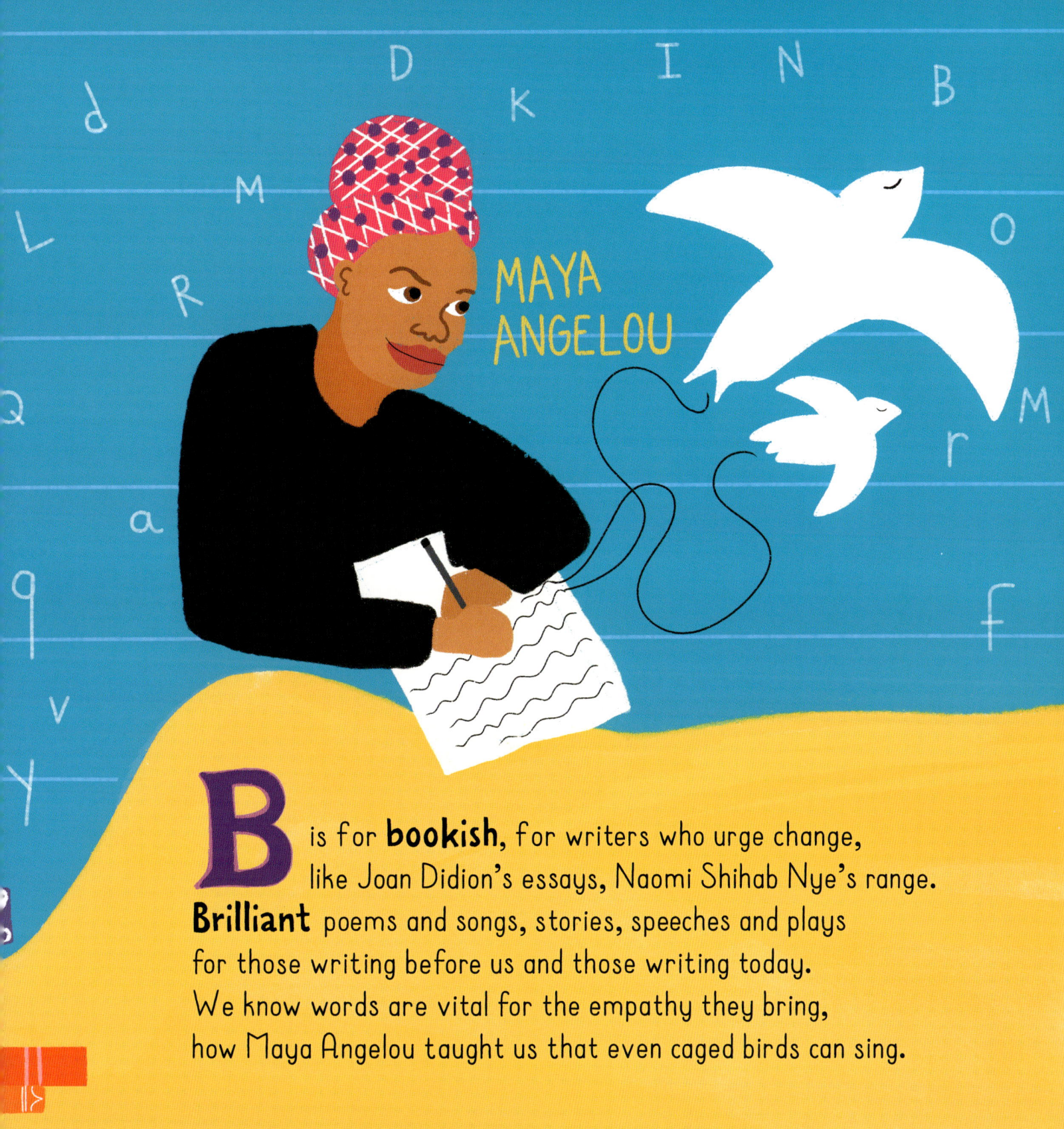

MAYA ANGELOU

B is for **bookish**, for writers who urge change,
like Joan Didion's essays, Naomi Shihab Nye's range.
Brilliant poems and songs, stories, speeches and plays
for those writing before us and those writing today.
We know words are vital for the empathy they bring,
how Maya Angelou taught us that even caged birds can sing.

C is for **Civil Rights**, it's for everyone's **choice**, and knowing when to speak out or quiet all the noise. The right to choose means choosing both what's right for you, and the **courage** to fight for others' rights too.

We have the right to our bodies, to education, and free speech, and the right to work at whatever we please.

MARY CASSATT

ZAHA HADID

ARTEMISIA GENTILESCHI

FAITH RINGGOLD

DIANE ARBUS

LOUISE BOURGEOIS

LEE KRASNER

ALMA THOMAS

AUGUSTA SAVAGE

EDMONIA LEWIS

D is for **dreaming** out loud and in color,
like the artists whose work helps us **discover**
there are new ways of seeing, more than one way to be.
We can imagine a world beyond you and me.
Alma Thomas's patterns, Frida Kahlo's reflections,
and Georgia O'Keeffe's florals teach beautiful lessons.
On canvas, in photographs, sculpted, or drawn,
art is what ensures the artist lives on,
and challenges each of us to create new **dawns**.

WANGARI MAATHAI

E is for **Earth,** she is Gaia, she is Mother.
We share the responsibility and work to protect her.
The water, air, soil, and each creature that roams—
our climate allows us to call this place home.
Greta Thunberg speaks for the air that we breathe.
Wangari Maathai was the "Mother of Trees."
Clean water to drink and healthy food to eat,
our **environment** connects us in more ways than we see.

ROSA PARKS

YURI
KOCHIYAMA

F is for **freedom fighters** like Yuri Kochiyama,
who organized movements and spoke truth to power.
By sharing her voice, her time, and her wisdom,
Rosa Parks showed us what freedom is and isn't.
These leaders blazed trails with their courage and vision.
The road may be tough, but we forge ahead on the mission.

ANGELA DAVIS

GRACE LEE BOGGS

MALALA YOUSAFZAI

G is for **groundbreakers** in science and math,
who did what they loved and so made a new path.

Katherine Johnson helped take us to space,
Virginia Apgar made sure babies were safe,
and the first programmer was Ada Lovelace.
With **gratitude** we use their discoveries today,
and thank them for ingeniously making a way.

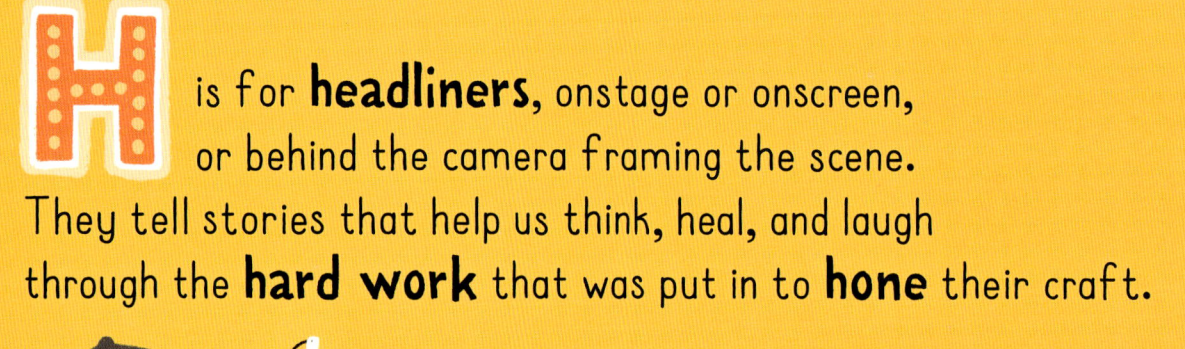

H is for **headliners,** onstage or onscreen,
or behind the camera framing the scene.
They tell stories that help us think, heal, and laugh
through the **hard work** that was put in to **hone** their craft.

EDITH HEAD

JULIE DASH

We **honor** those stars, and more we may yet know,
hopeful we all have our own role in the show.

I is for **intersectional**—a word **introduced** to show we're not just one thing. We contain multitudes!

MARSHA P. JOHNSON

J is for **justice**, seeking truth and support within a community or on the highest court.

SANDRA DAY O'CONNOR
FIRST WOMAN ON THE SUPREME COURT

RUTH BADER GINSBURG
FIRST JEWISH WOMAN ON THE SUPREME COURT

It's about balancing the scales, doing what's right and what's fair.
We've come a long way, baby, but we've got longer
to go before we're there.

SONIA SOTOMAYOR
FIRST LATINA WOMAN ON THE SUPREME COURT

KETANJI BROWN JACKSON
FIRST BLACK WOMAN ON THE SUPREME COURT

K is for **knowledge**—grown like a garden.
Who better to lead us than teachers and librarians?

Jean Blackwell Hutson

Pura Belpré

They cultivate how we learn, inform what we know.
We say THANK YOU for helping our understanding grow.
Jean Blackwell Hutson and Pura Belpré
looked at libraries and saw a new way.
Their kinship in building inclusive collections
now guides us in asking the important questions.

L is for **labor**, for the struggle for our work to be valued, to be **leaders**, who teach **lessons** and change points of view.
We fought for Paid Leave and for Equal Pay,
we fought to be heard when decisions are made.
Organizers planned and put our strength in numbers on display.
Dolores Huerta showed workers that yes, absolutely Si, Se Puede!

M is for **Ms.**—the first of its kind:
a magazine started by Gloria Steinem.
Ms. was a voice for women by women,
a voice that for years had been strategically hidden.
M is for **meticulous** writers who came before and came after,
who changed the whole discourse, not just their own chapters.

GLORIA STEINEM

Peace on earth
Goodwill to People

It's your year!

Women & money

Yes, we DO have women astronauts.

Sisterhood

IDA B. WELLS

SEXISM

RACISM

INVESTIGATIVE REPORTING

CIVIL RIGHTS

N is for No. Never again.

We are **Not** going backward. **Nope.**

FIGHT TODAY FOR A BETTER TOMORROW

BRIDGES NOT WALLS

CLIMATE JUSTICE NOW

THE FUTURE IS FEMME

WAR IS NOT THE ANSWER

PEACE NOW!

P is for **passion**, for **possible**, and for **pride**, for standing up for what you believe and setting challenges aside.

$$1+2=3$$

RUBY BRIDGES 1960

Passion

Principles are important, they make change and close rifts, and so many great stories begin *"She persists."*

Q is for **question.** Don't ever stop asking. Every detail deserves your attention.

The who, what, where, when, how, and why, with reflection, will always help point us in the right direction.

R is for **Riot Grrrls** and their **resourcefulness**,
who made their own way with laughter and forcefulness.
We can lift others up and work to fix what's broken,
but why not make some noise: If you care, be outspoken!

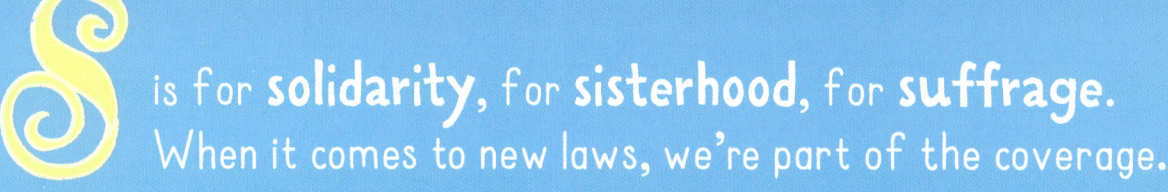

S is for **solidarity**, for **sisterhood**, for **suffrage**.
When it comes to new laws, we're part of the coverage.

The **Seneca Falls** gathering redefined our roles.
And years later, Ella Baker took up the fight for the polls.

CHLOE KIM

T is for **Title IX** making new women's **teams.**
Thanks to the law from Patsy Mink and Edith Green,
so many great athletes could finally be seen!
From **tenacious** beginners to winners of gold,
we're no longer sidelined, we play and we're bold.

U is for **unbought and unbossed!**
Shirley Chisholm's powerful slogan
brought women to office and set new laws in motion.

1942
BROOKLYN
COLLEGE

BROOKLYN, NY

1920s
SHIRLEY, A LEADER AMONG
HER FRIENDS.

V is for **vocalists** who gave us their songs—
these powerful anthems make us feel we belong.
Selena, Beyoncé, and Joni Mitchell, too,
offered joy and connection through their lasting tunes.

SELF-WORTH

LA FAMILIA

LOVE STORIES

SELENA

LA CHICANA MODERNA

JOY

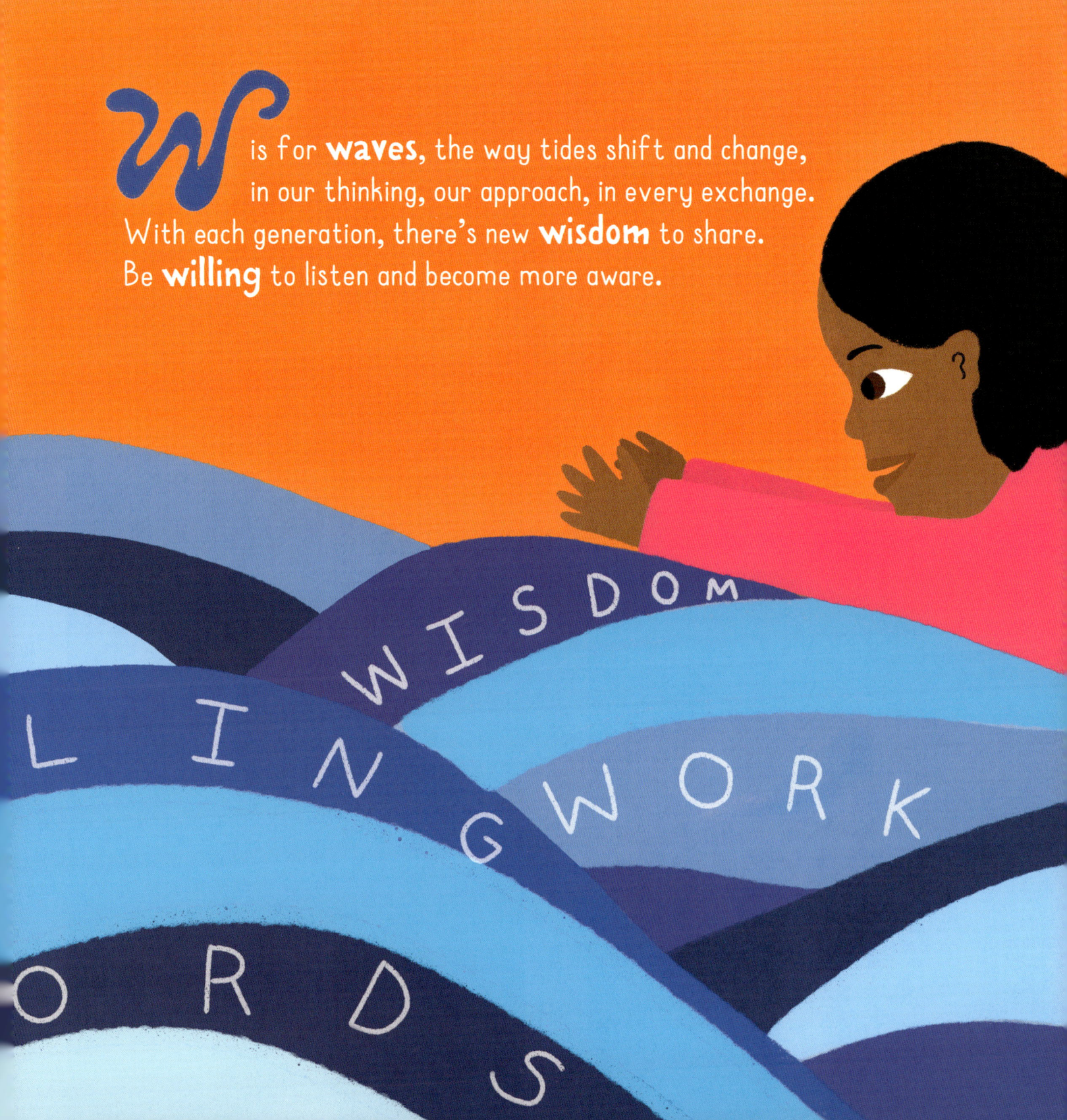

W is for **waves,** the way tides shift and change,
in our thinking, our approach, in every exchange.
With each generation, there's new **wisdom** to share.
Be **willing** to listen and become more aware.

MAE JEMISON

SALLY RIDE

HARRIET TUBMAN

AMERICA

ANNIE LONDONDERRY

FRANCE

EGYPT

SRI LANKA

JAPAN

X **marks the spot.** We have charted new ways:
We've been explorers, adventurers, the first, and the brave.
Mae Jemison and Sally Ride set their sights on the stars,
Annie Londonderry pedaled near and far,
Bessie Coleman dared to take to the skies,
and Harriet Tubman was a legendary liberator and guide.

QUEEN BESS

BESSIE COLEMAN

Y is for **you**. **Yes**, you, in all your glory. **You** are uniquely part of the story. There's a future ahead and a path to claim, and most important of all—a place for **your name.**

Z is for **zeal**, and the way history **zooms** before us.
As Zora Neale Hurston believed,
we are all part of that infinite, beautiful chorus.

I Am the past, present, and future.

The ABCs of Women's History: Terms and Figures

Women's history is a story of perseverance and wonder. And because women haven't always been recognized for their achievements, it is a story of named and unnamed heroes. Thanks to the work of women activists, community organizers, artists, and policymakers, we have made incredible strides toward equality and justice. Women's history is a rich tapestry of changemakers with different backgrounds, origins, and individual sets of challenges and triumphs. Women have changed the world and continue to move us forward today. Our story is a part of history that is so dynamic that it is impossible to capture all of its luminaries here, but here are a few women we hope inspire you, too.

June Jordan (1936–2002)

was an acclaimed Jamaican American poet, essayist, and writer. She wrote about subjects that were relevant to her survival: civil rights, women's rights, war, and the freedom to love whom you please. She wrote more than twenty-seven books and plays, and her work is shared widely today.

A is for Anew, Abundance, Affirmation

An **affirmation** is a statement of empowerment, positivity, or pride. "I am enough" is a common affirmation that expresses self-acceptance and self-worth. **Abundance** means more than enough—it means plenty. Throughout time, women have had to fight not only for their fundamental civil rights—with women of color often at the frontline—but also for the right to be seen, heard, and respected. Asserting that just as we are, we are *more* than enough, is a statement of our personal freedom and power.

It's our FUTURE

B is for Bookish, Brilliant

Women have been on the forefront of groundbreaking literature since the beginning of the written word, though not always given fair credit and the same opportunities to publish as male writers. **Anne Bradstreet (1612–1672)** was the first woman writer to publish from America. Originally born in Northamptonshire, England, Bradstreet moved to Massachusetts when she was 18 years old. In 1650, a book of her poems called *The Tenth Muse Lately Sprung Up in America* was published in England. More than a century later, in 1773, **Phillis Wheatley (1753–1784)**, born in West Africa and eventually enslaved in America, became the first African American, the first enslaved person, and the third woman in America to publish a book of poetry, *Poems on Various Subjects, Religious and Moral*. Many brilliant writers have followed in their footsteps, including:

Joan Didion (1934–2021) was a novelist and essayist. She wrote stories about California, where she was born and raised, and about the world. She was one of the pioneers of a style called New Journalism, which combines journalism and nonfiction narrative. Some of her most well-known books were *Slouching Toward Bethlehem* (1968) and *The Year of Magical Thinking* (2005), which won the National Book Award for nonfiction.

Naomi Shihab Nye (1952–) is an award-winning poet and writer who was born in St. Louis to a Palestinian father and American mother. She writes for both adults and children, and through her writing she has shown us unforgettable characters in everyday people. Her first poetry collection was called *Different Ways to Pray* (1980) and her first young adult novel was called *Habibi* (1997).

Maya Angelou (1928–2014) was a celebrated African American poet and memoirist who wrote many volumes of autobiography including her most famous work, *I Know Why the Caged Bird Sings* (1969). She was known not only for her award-winning writing, but also for her work during the Civil Rights Movement, her public conversations, and her art in other media such as dance and film.

C is for Civil Rights, Courage

Civil rights issues affect everyone. Some of the rights that women have courageously fought for include the right to an education, the right to earn an equal wage, the right to own property, the right to vote, and the right to choose whether or when to have children. One of the efforts to secure women's rights was known as the **Women's Liberation Movement**, which took place in the 1960s and 1970s; women sought maternity leave rights, equal job training, and laws banning employment discrimination, as well as greater personal freedom.

The Third World Women's Alliance (1968–1980), established around the same time as the Women's Liberation Movement, was a revolutionary group of women of color. They took one of the earliest approaches to intersectionality (see the letter "I" below)—seeking liberation for all women.

D is for Dreaming, Discover

There is a rich legacy of women visual artists and painters.

Alma Woodsey Thomas (1891–1978) was a major American painter and teacher celebrated for her vibrant, detailed, and colorful works. As an African American woman, she achieved success in the face of segregation and prejudice. She was the first graduate of Howard University's art department.

Frida Kahlo (1907–1954) was a renowned Mexican and feminist painter known best for self-portraits, many of which she painted after she was seriously injured in a bus accident. While her work remained lesser-known until the 1970s, long after her death, she is now one of the most internationally celebrated icons in art history.

Georgia O'Keeffe (1887–1986) was a painter best known for her depictions of enlarged flowers and landscapes from the American Southwest. Because of her unique style and new way of painting nature, she played an important role in the growth of modern art in America. She is known as one of the most significant painters of the twentieth century.

E is for Earth, Environment

Women have always been on the frontlines of movements to protect the environment, and their efforts have made and continue to make significant changes for our planet. The modern environmental movement in America began in the 1960s, amid rising concerns about air and water pollution.

Gaia was the ancient Greek goddess of Earth, mother of all life. There are many cultural equivalents to Gaia, including the Roman goddess **Terra Mater** and others that pre-date Gaia in the non-Western world. Mother Earth is home to the arc of all human history.

Greta Thunberg (2003–) is a Swedish environmental activist who has challenged world leaders to take action on climate change. When she was only 15, she began a student-led walkout movement called Fridays for Future, during which weekly student protests brought attention to climate change and inspired climate activists of all ages—but especially younger generations—to get involved.

Wangari Muta Maathai (1940–2011) was a Kenyan environmental and political activist and the first African woman to receive the Nobel Peace Prize. She launched the **Green Belt Movement**, which focused on the planting of trees, conservation, and women's rights. She became known as "Mama Miti," which translates to "Mother of Trees."

Another important name in environmental activism is **Tara Houska**, a tribal attorney, land defender, and climate justice activist. A member of Couchiching First Nation (her Native name is Zhaabowekwe), she was active in the resistance against multiple oil pipelines, including the Dakota Access pipeline, and has been deeply involved in the movement to defund fossil fuels.

F is for Freedom Fighters

The path toward justice and equality is never easy. Many inspiring women throughout history have fought for the expansion of rights and opportunities for all of us.

Angela Davis (1944 –) is a scholar, activist, writer, and lifelong advocate for the oppressed. She argues for the abolition of prisons and was involved with the Black Panther Party. She has written many books, including *Women, Race & Class* (1981) and *Are Prisons Obsolete?* (2003).

Yuri Kochiyama (1921 –2014) was a Japanese American civil rights activist whose family's time in an American internment camp during WWII was an early influence on her political activism. She lived for many years in Harlem, New York, where she joined the Civil Rights Movement as well as antinuclear efforts. She later fought for the passage of the **Civil Liberties Act of 1988**, which granted reparations to every living Japanese American who had survived their forced internment by the US government. She used that victory in her fight for reparations for the descendants of enslaved Americans.

Rosa Parks (1913 –2005) was an American civil rights activist, and the United States Congress has honored her as the "mother of the freedom movement." In 1955, she boarded a bus in Montgomery, Alabama, and instead of heading to the back of the bus, which was designated for African Americans, she remained seated toward the front. When asked by the bus driver to move, she refused, setting in motion the **Montgomery Bus Boycott**, one of America's most significant protests.

Grace Lee Boggs (1915 –2015) was a Chinese American philosopher whose activism spanned several major social movements of the 20th century. She fought for workers' rights, civil rights, women's rights, and environmental justice.

Malala Yousafzai (1997 –) is an education activist from Pakistan. At age seventeen, she became the youngest Nobel Peace Prize laureate in history.

G is for Groundbreakers

Women's contributions in science and math have created enormous advancements in the fields of medicine, engineering, and technology. Not only did women have to fight just to study and participate in these fields, they went on to make life-changing discoveries and continue to do so today.

Katherine Johnson (1918 –2020) was a Black American mathematician and author. She made important contributions to the US space program through her calculations and helped astronauts go to the moon.

Virginia Apgar (1909 –1974) was an American physician who is best known for inventing the Apgar Score, which is a method to assess the health of a newborn baby. This quick test is still routinely used today.

Ada Lovelace (1815 –1852) was an English mathematician who is widely known as one of the first computer programmers. Her contributions to computer science were not discovered until the 1950s, but she is thought to have written the first line of computer code.

H is for Headliners, Hard Work

While women didn't always have control of their images or the way they were represented in film, women on screen and behind the camera have worked to transform representation and storytelling.

Edith Head (1897 –1981) was an American costume designer who started as an artist for Paramount Studios in 1923. She became the most awarded woman in the history of the Academy Awards, nominated 35 times and winning eight Oscars for Best Costume Design.

Julie Dash (1952 –) is a director whose best-known movie, *Daughters of the Dust* (1991), was the first full-length film directed by a Black woman to have a US theatrical release. Throughout her career, she has created work that centers Black women's stories in a way they have never before been portrayed on film.

Rita Moreno (1931 –) is a Puerto Rican actor, dancer, and singer. She was the first Latina to win all of the major entertainment awards—an Emmy, Grammy, Oscar, and Tony. Her career in the entertainment industry has spanned more than eight decades.

Anna May Wong (1905 –1961) was the first Chinese American Hollywood movie star. She broke barriers in representation, but even so, she became weary of being cast in stereotypical roles, and shifted from film to activism later in her career.

Meryl Streep (1949 –) is an award-winning American actor known for her portrayal of female characters who are complex and dynamic.

In a career spanning nearly 70 years, **Cicely Tyson (1924–2021)** insisted on roles that portrayed the dignity, power, and resilience of Black women. She won a Tony Award for Best Actress at age 88—the oldest actress ever to receive that award.

Ve Neill (born Mary Flores, 1951–) is an American makeup artist. She has won three Academy Awards for her work, and has created some of the most iconic character appearances in film over the last several decades, including Beetlejuice and Batman.

I is for Intersectional

Intersectionality is an idea that was first introduced by **Kimberlé Crenshaw (1959 –)**, an American civil rights advocate and scholar. Each person in this world has many identities, like gender, race, nationality, religion, or ability. Dr. Crenshaw's concept of intersectionality speaks to how these different identities combine to create different realities in the world and acknowledges the impact of those unique identities.

Marsha P. Johnson (1945 –1992) was pivotal in the gay rights movement. She spoke up for houseless LGBTQIA+ youth as well as transgender rights and was a prominent figure in the **Stonewall Uprising** of 1969. Along with Sylvia Rivera, she exemplified what it means to advocate across gender, sexuality, and racial identities.

Sylvia Rivera (1951–2002) was a community organizer and activist who fought to make sure transgender people and people of color were included in the gay rights movement. She also took part in the **Stonewall Uprising**.

J is for Justice

The Supreme Court is the highest court in the United States. **Sandra Day O'Connor (1930 –2023)** became the first female justice of the Supreme Court in 1981. In 1993, **Ruth Bader Ginsburg (1933 –2020)** became the second woman and the first Jewish woman appointed to the court. In 2009, **Sonia Sotomayor (1954 –)** became the first woman of color and the first Latina Supreme Court justice. And, in 2022, **Ketanji Brown Jackson (1970 –)** became the first Black woman ever appointed to the Supreme Court.

"You've come a long way, baby" is one of the most famous advertising slogans in history. Used by a cigarette brand to target female customers, it referenced advancements made in the women's liberation movement in the 1960s and 1970s.

K is for Knowledge

Women have contributed greatly to the field of library science, the archives of knowledge. Librarians are often the keepers and curators of our most important stories. Here are just a couple of legendary women librarians:

Pura Belpré (1899 –1982) was an Afro-Puerto Rican educator, librarian, and children's author. She was the first Puerto Rican librarian in New York City, and she pioneered outreach from the library to the Caribbean community. In 1996, the Pura Belpré Award was established in her name, honoring Latine authors and illustrators who celebrate and affirm the Latine cultural experience.

Jean Blackwell Hutson (1914 –1998) was an African American educator, librarian, and activist who served most of her career at the Schomburg Center for Research in Black Culture in Harlem, New York, eventually becoming their chief curator. She shared Arturo Schomburg's vision that Black history was worth preserving, and that we must rebuild the past to create a new future.

L is for Labor, Leaders

Women have had to fight for their work to be valued equally, both at home and in the workplace. In 1963, Congress passed the **Equal Pay Act**, making it illegal for employers to discriminate on wages on the basis of sex. And, in 1993, a law called the **Family and Medical Leave Act** ensured that workers have job protection while they care for family members, from newborn babies to parents.

Clara Lemlich Shavelson (1886 –1982) was a garment worker and union organizer in New York City who helped lead the 1909 **Uprising of the 20,000**, the largest strike at that time by women workers. The strike created safer workplaces and forced male union leadership to change their prejudice against striking women.

Addie L. Wyatt (1924 –2012) was the first woman to become president of a local union. She co-founded the Coalition of Labor Union Women (CLUW) and the National Organization of Women (NOW), and she helped redefine women's roles in the labor movement forever.

Dolores Huerta (1930 –) is a labor activist and co-founder of the United Farm Workers Association (UFWA). During her organizing efforts, she coined the phrase "Sí, se puede!" ("Yes, we can!") to encourage laborers to unionize and create demands, and it became a rallying cry for the labor movement as a whole.

M is for *Ms.*

Ms. **magazine** was the first feminist magazine in the United States, founded in 1971 by activist and writer **Gloria Steinem** at the encouragement of African American activist **Dorothy Pitman Hughes**.

Gloria Steinem (1934 –) is a feminist, activist, and trailblazing journalist who has been a pivotal, highly visible spokesperson for the women's rights movement throughout her career.

Dorothy Pitman Hughes (1938 –2022) was a public speaker, child welfare advocate, and

feminist. She spoke up about the need for the feminist movement to address racism among white women.

Ida B. Wells (1862 –1931) was a journalist and civil rights activist. Born enslaved, Wells was emancipated after the Civil War and became one of the co-founders of the National Association for the Advancement of Colored People (NAACP). Her journalism exposed the realities of Reconstruction-era life for many Black Americans.

Susan Sontag (1933 –2004) was an award-winning American writer and political activist. She is best known for her writing about culture and human rights. She traveled to places across the globe that had seen conflict and war, and covered subjects ranging from the Vietnam War and the Bosnian War to photography and the AIDS crisis in America.

Nikole Hannah-Jones (1976 –) is an investigative journalist who often covers racial injustice and civil rights. She won the Pulitzer Prize for commentary in 2020 for her work on *The 1619 Project*, a *New York Times* series marking the 400th anniversary of slavery in America. Her reporting sought to explore the history of slavery and the founding of the United States and to show the connections between them.

N is for Never Again

"Abortion Victims: **Never Again**" was the title of a groundbreaking article mourning the women who had died in need of abortions, written by Roberta Brandes Gratz and published in *Ms.* magazine in 1973, the same year that *Roe v. Wade* was decided. "Never Again" became a motto of the reproductive rights movement for years to come.

Roe v. Wade was a landmark ruling of the US Supreme Court protecting a pregnant person's constitutional liberty to obtain an abortion. This ruling was overturned by the Supreme Court in 2022.

O is for Outspoken, Organize

There is a long tradition of community organizing in women's history, as well as numerous organizations that support communities of women.

P is for Passion, Pride, Principles, Persist

Throughout history, persistence, passion, and principles have driven ideas forward and made change possible for women.

Ruby Bridges (1954 –) is an American Civil Rights activist. Prior to 1954, many US schools were segregated by race, with white children attending some schools and Black children attending others. The US Supreme Court decided in ***Brown vs. Board of Education*** (1954) that Black and white children would attend school together. In 1960, Bridges became the first African American student to integrate into an all-white elementary school in the US.

Kamala Harris (1964 –) became the first woman, the first Black American, and the first South Asian American vice president of the United States on January 20, 2021. She entered politics in 1990, and she is a lawyer. It took sixty-one years for equal representation in schools to lead to representation in the second highest office in the United States.

"***Nevertheless, she persisted***" are the words that the then-Senate majority leader spoke in reference to Senator Elizabeth Warren after the US Senate voted to silence her during a 2017 confirmation hearing. The phrase gained greater meaning as it became representative of women breaking barriers and speaking out, even after being historically silenced or ignored.

Q is for Question

Asking questions is an essential part of understanding, progress, and history. Questioning the status quo is the first step many women have taken toward later fights for more fair and equal treatment. Questions are an important part of how we create empathy and understand one another, and asking them is a simple practice that enriches both our lives and the story of women's history.

R is for Riot Grrrls, Resourcefulness

The **Riot Grrrl Movement** was an underground feminist punk movement that began in the 1990s as a reaction to sexism in the punk scene. Though it started in the Pacific Northwest, the movement spread around the globe.

Bikini Kill was a punk band formed in Olympia, Washington, in 1990 and widely considered to be a pioneer of the Riot Grrrl Movement. The group was made up of vocalist and songwriter **Kathleen Hanna (1968 –)**, bassist **Kathi Wilcox (1969 –)**, guitarist **Billy Karren (1965 –)**, and drummer **Tobi Vail (1969 –)**.

In addition to music, the Riot Grrrl Movement included a creative subculture with a DIY (Do It Yourself) attitude and perspective, involving zine-making and other grassroots actions. It was an accessible style, open to all.

Ramdasha Bikceem (1970s –) is an American writer and musician who published the trailblazing Riot Grrrl zine *GUNK*, which addressed racism, feminism, skateboarding, and music.

S is for Solidarity, Sisterhood, Suffrage

Suffrage means "the right to vote." Women fought for decades to claim this right, which was finally guaranteed with the 1920 ratification of the 19th Amendment. Even though Black men had gained suffrage after the Civil War with the passage of the 15th Amendment in 1870, racist efforts and tactics to suppress the Black vote never ceased. Civil rights activists fought hard to bring attention to this injustice, and, in 1965, the federal **Voting Rights Act** was passed, prohibiting racial discrimination in voting.

Elizabeth Cady Stanton (1815 –1902) was a leader in the women's rights and suffrage movements. She was an abolitionist and writer,

and one of the minds behind the historic **Seneca Falls Convention**, which was the first women's rights convention and took place in Seneca Falls, New York, in 1848.

Sojourner Truth (1797–1883) was born enslaved and became an outspoken abolitionist, women's and civil rights activist, and author. She dictated her autobiography, *The Narrative of Sojourner Truth* (1850), and in 1851 delivered what would become a famous speech, **"Ain't I a Woman?,"** which challenged prevalent attitudes of both racism and sexism.

Ella Baker (1903–1986) was an icon of the voting rights movement. She was a grassroots organizer who played important roles in the NAACP, the Student Nonviolent Coordinating Committee (SNCC), and Martin Luther King Jr.'s Southern Christian Leadership Conference (SCLC). She worked toward justice for many decades.

Fannie Lou Hamer (1917–1977) was a civil rights activist instrumental in ensuring Black people's right to vote in the United States. Her organizing efforts were part of the force that led to the passing of the Voting Rights Act of 1965.

T is for Title IX, Teams

Title IX prohibits sex discrimination in all federally funded educational programs, including sports.

Patsy Mink (1927–2002) was the first woman of color and first Asian American woman elected to Congress, serving as a representative from Hawai'i from 1965–1977 and from 1990–2002. **Edith Green (1910–1987)** was a member of the US House of Representatives for Oregon from 1954 to 1974. After Mink co-authored the Title IX Amendment of the Higher Education Act, Green was instrumental in passing it. It was signed into law in 1972 and renamed the Patsy T. Mink Equal Opportunity in Education Act in 2002.

Ibtihaj Muhammad (1985–) is a five-time World medalist and World Champion in sabre fencing. In 2016, she became the first American woman to compete in the Olympics in hijab and the first Muslim American woman to win an Olympic medal.

Chloe Kim (2000–) is a Korean American snowboarder. At age seventeen, she was the youngest woman in Olympic history to win a gold medal in the halfpipe event.

The Williams sisters are American tennis legends who broke down racial barriers in the sport. They are both four-time Olympic gold medalists. **Venus Williams (1980–)** is a seven-time Grand Slam title winner. **Serena Williams (1981–)** is a twenty-three-time Grand Slam title winner, and widely thought of as one of the greatest athletes of all time.

Billie Jean King (1943–) is a former American tennis player who has won thirty-nine major titles. She spent her career advocating for equality in women's sports and was outspoken in the passing of Title IX.

After their World Cup victory in 2019, the **US Women's National Soccer Team** still had to fight to be paid the same amount as the US Men's National Team. Outspoken team members like **Megan Rapinoe (1985–)** and **Alex Morgan (1989–)** helped spread word about the pay discrepancy. In 2023, President Joe Biden signed the **Equal Pay for Team USA** law, which requires that all athletes representing the United States in global competition receive equal pay and benefits.

U is for "Unbought and Unbossed"

Shirley Chisholm (1924–2005) was the first Black woman elected to Congress, and, in 1972, became the first Black woman to seek a major party's nomination to run for president of the United States. Her iconic campaign slogan was "Unbought and Unbossed," reminding voters of her individualism and independence. She paved the way for women to continue to join Congress.

V is for Vocalists

Women singers and songwriters have long used their voices to create anthems, inspire change, and give power to the voiceless.

Selena Quintanilla Pérez (1971–1995) was known to the world as Selena and the "Queen of Tejano Music." She is one of the most celebrated Mexican American recording artists of our time and was poised to break out as a global star in the music industry when her life was tragically cut short.

Beyoncé Giselle Knowles-Carter (1981–) is an American singer and songwriter, known widely as "Queen Bey." She's used her platform and themes of empowerment in her music to impact and shift the cultural conversation. She is considered one of the greatest entertainers of her generation.

Joni Mitchell (1943–) is a Canadian singer, songwriter, and painter. She is one of the most influential musicians to arise from the 1960s folk music circuit and is known for her poetic lyrical style.

W is for Waves, Wisdom

One way of thinking about different feminist movements in the United States is as waves. Each wave of feminism reignited the conversation about women's rights, and feminism became more inclusive and relevant to the changing times with each turn. The **First Wave** is considered to have taken place from 1848 to 1920, the **Second Wave** from 1963 to the 1980s, the **Third Wave** from the 1990s onward, and the **Fourth Wave** is happening today. These waves don't capture all of the nuances and distinctions in feminism, but it is one way to think about the incredible story of women's movements in the United States.

X is for X Marks the Spot

Women have indeed always charted new paths and been the first to reach new frontiers in many fields. Here are just a few of the women who challenged not only the physical expectations of their time, but also what was possible, setting new records and accomplishing firsts in flight, space, and travels.

Mae Jemison (1956–) is an astronaut and the first Black American woman to travel into space.

Sally Ride (1951–2012) was a physicist and the first American woman in space.

Annie Londonderry (1870–1947) was a Jewish Latvian American cyclist who became the first woman to travel around the world by bicycle.

Bessie Coleman (1892–1926) was the first Black and first Indigenous woman to earn a pilot's license in the United States. She was known as "Brave Bessie."

Harriet Tubman (ca. 1822–1913) was an enslaved woman who liberated herself and freed at least seventy others. Tubman was a conductor in the Underground Railroad, a network of safe houses where the enslaved hid as they escaped to free territory. During the Civil War, Tubman also spied for the Union (Northern) Army. In 1863, she helped lead a secret mission on the Combahee River in South Carolina that freed more than 700 enslaved people.

Y is for You

Each of us has a place in history as it is being made, and we are each part of the context of the history that came before us. That includes you, Reader.

Z is for Zeal

Zeal means enthusiasm or passion. History is all around us, and the ways that women have shaped history continue to affect us today. Whether you're inspired by figures from this book and beyond or ancestors of your own, we all move forward on the wings of the past, and we each have an impact on the way history marches ahead.

Zora Neale Hurston (1891–1960) was an anthropologist and one of the preeminent women writers of the twentieth century, Her work often centered Black life in the American South and Black folklore. Her most famous work is a novel, *Their Eyes Were Watching God* (1937).

RIO CORTEZ

is a Harlem-based writer whose work has appeared in *The New Yorker*, *The Atlantic*, *The Miami Rail*, and many other publications. She is also the author of the *New York Times* bestselling title *The ABCs of Black History* and *The River Is My Ocean*, as well as the adult poetry collection *Golden Ax*, which was longlisted for a National Book Award. Visit her website at riocortez.com.

LAUREN SEMMER

is a Manhattan-based artist and designer whose work has been featured in the *New York Times*, *The Washington Post*, and *Real Simple* magazine. She is the illustrator of the *New York Times* bestselling title *The ABCs of Black History*, also written by Rio Cortez, and the Bank Street College of Education "Best Book" *To Boldly Go: How Nichelle Nichols and Star Trek Helped Advance Civil Rights*. Her author-illustrator debut is *Poppy's Family Patterns*. Visit her website at laurensemmer.com.

WITH THANKS

Rio and Lauren are grateful to all the groundbreaking women who came before them, paving paths for them to be both artists and mothers, and hope their work will, even in some small way, clear obstacles for future generations of women.